$ 11.90

S0-DHU-813

Snails

First Steck-Vaughn Edition 1992

This book has been reviewed
for accuracy by
David Skryja
Associate Professor of Biology
University of Wisconsin Center—Waukesha.

Library of Congress Cataloging in Publication Data

Oda, Hidetomo.
  Snails.

  (Nature close-ups)
  Translation of: Katatsumuri / text by Hidetomo Oda,
photographs by Nanao Kikaku.
  Summary: Text and photographs describe the life
cycle, behavior, and natural habitat of various kinds
of snails.
  1. Snails—Juvenile literature.   [1. Snails]
I. Nanao Kikaku (Firm) II. Title. III. Series.
QL430.4.03513 1986   594'3   85-28211

ISBN 0-8172-2544-7 (lib. bdg.)
ISBN 0-8172-2569-2 (softcover)

This edition first published in 1986 by Raintree Publishers Inc.,
a Division of Steck-Vaughn Company.

  3 4 5 6 7 8 9 0   95 94 93 92 91

Snails

RAINTREE
STECK-VAUGHN
L I B R A R Y
A Division of Steck-Vaughn Company

▶ **Snail in the rain.**

During cold winter weather, snails remain inactive, in a state of hibernation. But in spring, the warm rains bring snails out of their long hibernation.

◀ **A snail sliding along a hydrangea leaf.**

When snails come out of hibernation, they are very hungry because they haven't eaten all winter. Most land snails eat tender new plant leaves or tree buds, but some also eat decaying plant material.

Many of nature's creatures seek shelter from the rain, and some are even endangered by it, but snails are just the opposite. Look for them on rainy days, or in damp, shady places, or at night when everything is covered with dew.

There are many kinds of snails throughout the world. In fact, there are more than 80,000 species. Some are about the size of the period at the end of this sentence. Others measure two feet in length. Some snails live only a short time, and some live as long as twenty years. Most snails carry their "houses" with them. These are beautifully marked shells. There are land snails and water snails, but scientists believe all snails lived under water at one time. That is because all snails have one thing in common—they must keep their bodies cool and moist or they will die.

● Cone-shaped spirals form the snail's protective shell.

Snails belong to a large group of animals called mollusks. Mollusks have soft bodies, which are usually protected by a hard shell. Some mollusks, like oysters, mussels, and clams, develop two hinged shells. But snails form only one.

A snail's shell grows in a fascinating way. A thin skin called a mantle covers the top part of the snail's body beneath the shell. Certain glands in the mantle use chemicals from the food and water consumed by the snail to produce the hard shell material. As new shell material is produced, cone-shaped spirals, or whorls, are formed, and the shell grows larger. The shell protects the snail's body from enemies, or predators.

◄ **A snail stretching its tentacles.**

Most land snails have two pairs of tentacles. At the tip of the longer tentacles, there are black eyes. The eyes can sense light and dark but cannot tell the shapes of things. The shorter tentacles are sensitive to touch and help the snail feel its way along.

▼ **Snails stretching their bodies.**

Because the snail has no bones, its body is very pliable. When it goes into its shell, the shell covers and protects the entire body of the snail.

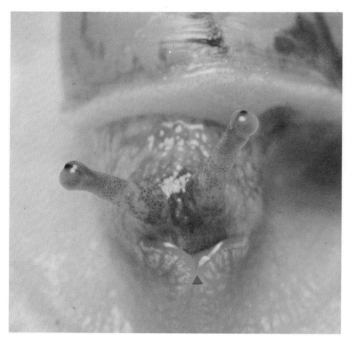

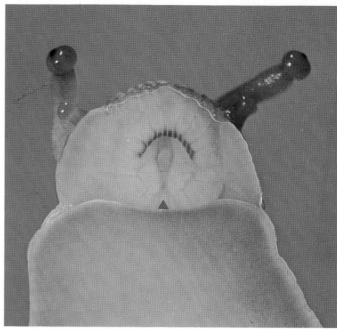

▲ **The front of a snail's head.**

The snail's mouth (arrow) is located beneath its shorter tentacles. The snail uses its short tentacles to detect food. Although its tentacles may look like ears, the snail cannot hear sounds at all.

▲ **Close-up of a snail's mouth.**

The roundish tongue in the snail's mouth is visible here. The radula has tiny teeth, which shred food into particles that the snail can digest.

The snail's crescent-shaped mouth is located on the underside of its head. Its long, flat tongue, called a radula, has many rows of tiny, sharp teeth. When the snail rubs its radula along the surface of a leaf, it saws back and forth, shredding the leaf to pieces. It then pulls the shredded material into its mouth and begins to digest the food.

Land snails feed mostly on plant leaves and tree buds, as well as on decaying vegetation. Snails that live in ponds, rivers, and lakes eat water plants and dead animals. There are even some ocean snails that attach themselves to other sea animals and live off their flesh.

▶ Damage to crops.

Snails also eat vegetables. Snails may cause damage to cucumbers and other crops.

▼ A snail eating a leaf.

The land snail's main source of food is plant leaves. The snail holds the leaf with its large flat foot as it chews the leaf.

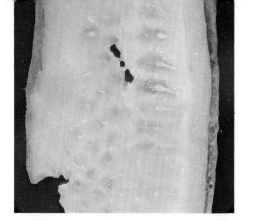

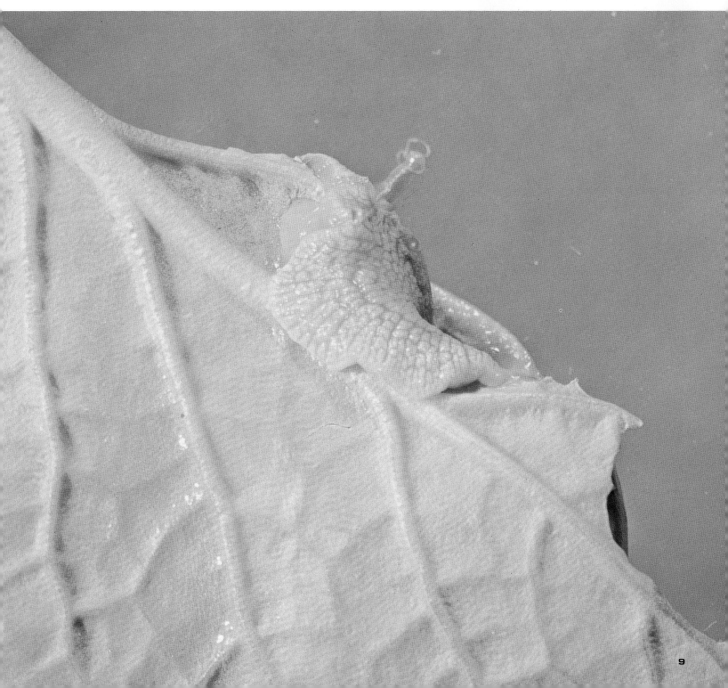

◀ **A snail gliding along a leaf.**

As it moves, the snail's foot secretes a sticky fluid which makes the snail adhere to the leaf. That is why the snail does not fall off when it is upside down on a leaf.

▶ **The bottom of a snail's foot.**

In this photo, the snail is on a piece of glass. You can see its entire foot. The faint lines going across the bottom of the foot are caused by the muscle contractions that move the snail forward.

The land snail glides with great ease over plant leaves, along thin vines, and up tree trunks. It is the snail's foot which makes it such a good traveler. The foot is the largest part of the snail's body that is outside its shell. It is a long, flat piece of tissue that has many powerful muscles. The muscles contract in waves from the back to the front of the foot, enabling the snail to move forward in a slow, gliding fashion. The front of the snail's foot secretes a slippery substance, mucus, that makes it easier for the snail to glide along.

▲ A snail climbing a mountain of pencils.

This snail uses its short tentacles to feel its way over a group of colored pencils. It leaves a trail of mucus behind it.

Scientists call snails and other related mollusks gastropods. The name comes from two Greek words meaning "belly" and "foot." Snails are called gastropods because they seem to crawl along on their bellies.

Of course it is actually the snail's foot, spread beneath its body, which moves it along. When the foot is fully extended, the snail seems to be twice as long as it is when the foot is curled inside its shell.

At the front end of the foot is the snail's head, complete with mouth, eyes, and tentacles, but no ears. The snail's other body organs (heart, kidneys, stomach and so forth) are located in a kind of hump inside the shell.

▶ A snail climbing a string.

By wrapping its flat foot tightly around the string, the snail can inch its way up. The snail moves very slowly—at a "snail's pace."

▼ Snails crossing a tightrope.

Because its shell is large and heavy in proportion to its small body, the snail has trouble keeping its balance. The snail on the bottom rope finds it easier to keep its balance with its shell hanging down.

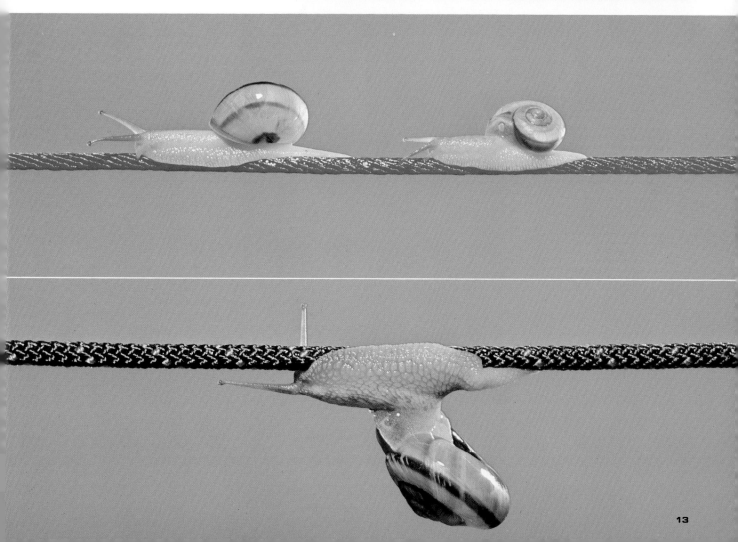

◄ **Snails during courtship.**

Land snails have unusual court-ship ceremonies. One snail will circle another. Sometimes two snails will rub their heads together, then their feet, to get to know each other.

▶ **Snails mating.**

When snails mate, they ex-change deposits of sperm through an opening near the head called the genital pore. Each snail's eggs are then fertilized in its body.

As many other animals do, land snails instinctively mate in the spring of the year. Snails reproduce in a most unusual way. There are no male or female snails. Each snail has characteristics of both sexes. Even though a snail can produce both eggs and sperm in its body, it still needs to mate for baby snails to be born. A snail's eggs must be joined with another snail's sperm. So, when it comes time to mate, snails, like other animals, look for partners.

Snails search for mates of their own kind, or species. After the courtship, snails mate by exchanging sperm. Inside each snail's body, the sperm unite with the eggs, and the mating process is complete.

▲ A snail burrowing beneath leaves.

Usually, the snail picks a damp, rainy time to lay its eggs. Hidden beneath moist earth or damp foliage, the eggs are protected from enemies and are kept from drying out in the sun.

After a month has passed, the snail is ready to lay its eggs. Many land snails lay their eggs in damp soil. Others deposit eggs under rocks or dead leaves or beneath tree bark. After the snail finds a suitable place, it digs a shallow hole. Then it passes the eggs through the genital pore and deposits them in the hole. The number of eggs laid depends on the species of snail. There may be fifty to several hundred tiny, rubbery eggs in a cluster. After the snail has laid its eggs, it covers them with dirt and smooths over the nest. The eggs are then left on their own to develop and hatch.

● **A snail laying eggs.**

After the eggs are deposited in a cool, damp place, they are left to develop on their own. Inside each egg, a tiny embryo is growing. The yolk of the egg furnishes the developing baby snail with food. The egg's tough, jelly-like covering protects the tiny snail inside.

17

▲ **Snail eggs ready to hatch.**

Nourished by the egg's yolk, the baby snail grows rapidly. In warm weather, an egg is hatched twenty to thirty days after it has been laid. If the weather is colder, it might take more than forty days for an egg to hatch.

It takes about a month for the baby snail inside the egg to develop fully. The time varies somewhat, depending on the species of snail and on the weather conditions. When the egg is ready to hatch, the snail's shell can be seen through the transparent, jelly-like walls of the egg. The baby snail hatches from the egg with its soft, thin, tiny shell intact. At first, the shell is only about a spiral and a half around, and it is light in color.

▲ This newborn snail is almost fully emerged from the eggshell.

◄ Birth of a snail (photos 1-4).

When cracks appear in the egg, the snail is ready to hatch. (1) The cracked egg splits open, and the soft, newly formed shell of the baby snail becomes visible. (2) Then the head appears, complete with two pairs of tentacles, with eyes already developed at the tips of the longer pair. (3) The snail's head seems very large compared to the rest of its tiny body. (4) The shells of these newborn snails are only about a spiral and a half around.

◄ A baby snail on a flax plant.

Soft flowers are the best food for the baby snail. If you look closely, you can see the muscles which move the tentacles in this baby snail.

► A baby snail searching for food.

This baby snail's shell has grown larger and darker. The snail spends the hot days in the shade and comes out at night, or on rainy days, in search of food.

When the snail is first born, it looks very much like an adult, except that it is much smaller and its shell is transparent.

Its first meal is usually its own empty eggshell. But the baby snail soon crawls from the place where it was hatched, in search of other food. It looks for soft flowers and tender new plant leaves.

The hot, dry winds of summer can quickly dry out the baby snail's soft, thin shell. The young snail must eat a lot and grow very quickly so that its shell will grow larger and harder to protect it from the hot summer weather.

In some countries, like Japan, the singing of the cicada announces that the rainy season is over and the hot season is about to begin.

▼ **A snail attached to a tree branch.**

During the hot summer, snails seek shade beneath branches on trees, under grass and leaves, and in damp places.

During the hot summer, the snail often stays in its shell for protection from the harsh sun. Once it has pulled its body inside, the snail secretes a sticky fluid, mucus, which seals the opening of the shell. This keeps the moisture from escaping to the outside. Inside, the snail stays cool and moist as it patiently waits for better weather. During dry weather, a snail may stay in its shell for several months. Its body functions slow down and it lives on stored energy during this time. Scientists call this period of inactivity estivation. Snails often attach themselves to tree trunks during estivation because it is safer for them to be off the ground.

▼ **A snail in estivation.** When it finds a shady spot on a tree, the snail secretes a sticky substance which allows it to adhere to the tree. It is safer for the snail to sleep for long periods of time high up off the ground.

● **A ground beetle attacking a snail.**

This ground beetle reaches deep inside a cracked snail shell as it feasts on the snail's body.

▲ **A firefly larva attacking a snail.**

This firefly larva wraps itself around the snail shell as it stings its victim, paralyzing it.

The snail retreats into its shell for protection from its enemies, as well as to escape from very hot or very cold weather. But its shell cannot protect the land snail from all who hunt, or prey, upon it. Ground beetles and firefly larvae are two of the snail's worst predators. The ground beetle's strong jaws can easily crack open a snail's shell. The beetle's long, narrow head can reach deep into the shell to find its prey. And some species of firefly larvae inject a poisonous liquid into the snail which paralyzes it and liquefies its body. The larva then sucks up its dinner.

◀ **A snail's respiratory pore.**

Oxygen passes to the land snail's lungs through an opening called the respiratory pore. It is located under the edge of the snail's shell, where the mantle forms a fold or collar.

▶ **Leaves changing color.**

The snail must eat as many green leaves as possible before they change color and fall from the trees.

◀ **A snail eliminating waste.**

Close to the snail's respiratory pore is another hole, the anal opening, where waste materials leave the snail's body. The food taken in through the mouth is digested, and the waste passes out through the anal opening.

As the hot summer draws to a close and the cooler days of autumn approach, the land snail comes out of estivation. It then prepares for an even longer period of inactivity—hibernation through the cold winter. Autumn and winter are dangerous seasons for the snail. It must eat as much as possible before the leaves on the trees change color, so that it will have enough energy stored up to make it through the long winter. Once it begins to hibernate inside its shell, the snail will not eat anything for many months.

◀ **A snail preparing for winter.**

Burrowed in this nest of dry leaves, the snail prepares for winter. It has sealed the opening of its shell with a mucous membrane to keep out the cold.

▶ **A snail beneath the snow.**

This snail, snug in its sealed shell, is protected from the cold. The snail breathes through tiny air holes in the sealed membrane.

Before winter sets in, the snail looks for a safe place to hibernate. It may go beneath fallen leaves or on the underside of tree branches. When it has found a suitable place, the snail seals the opening of its shell with layers of mucus. It curls up far back inside the shell and stretches more and more layers of mucous membrane across the inner walls of the shell. Then it hibernates through the winter, living on stored energy, protected from the winter cold. The first warm rains of spring awaken the snail from its long sleep, and it will emerge from its shell once again.

Let's Find Out

How Are Water Snails Different from Land Snails?

▶ **A water snail.**

In the photo at the right, the snail's body is emerging from its shell. In the photo at the far right, the most visible part of the snail is its foot.

There are snails that live in the water and snails that live on land. Most water snails breathe through gills, as fish do. Land snails breathe with lungs, like people. But all snails have one thing in common—a need to stay cool and moist.

That is why scientists believe all snails lived in the water millions of years ago.

This type of water snail lives in freshwater ponds and lakes. Its flat foot and tentacles are very similar to those of the land snail.

Freshwater snails to land snails.

a mud snail   a marsh snail   a land snail   a snail   a slug

What Is a Slug?

A slug is a kind of land snail. Its body is similar to a snail's. But it does not have a shell, so it is able to creep easily underneath stones. Its lifestyle is similar to that of a snail's.

▲ A slug extending its tentacles.

▲ A slug's eggs.

Types of Snails

Snails have different patterns or shapes of shells depending on where they live.

a three-striped snail

a sinistral snail

a black rock snail

a land snail

a Japanese snail

a thin-shelled snail

a hairy snail

a lipstick snail

31

GLOSSARY

egg—a mature female germ cell. (pp. 15, 16)

estivation—a period of inactivity undergone by a snail during hot weather, when its body functions slow down. (pp. 22, 23, 27)

genital pore—an opening near the head through which snails exchange sperm. (p. 16)

hibernation—a period of inactivity undergone by animals during cold weather when their body functions slow down. (pp. 4, 27, 28)

mantle—a thin skin which lines the snail's shell. The mantle contains glands for producing new shell material. (pp. 6, 26)

mollusks—a group of soft-bodied animals without backbones, which usually live in shells, such as snails, oysters, clams. (p. 6)

radula—the snail's long, flat tongue which is covered with tiny teeth. (p. 8)

respiratory pore—a hole through which oxygen passes to the snail's lungs. (p. 26)

species—a group of animals which scientists have identified as having common traits. (pp. 4, 15, 16)

sperm—a mature male germ cell. (p. 15)

whorl—one of the turns, or coils, of a snail's shell. (p. 6)